An Up... Life

Written by Jo Windsor

PEARSON

Look at this sloth.
A sloth can go upside down.
A sloth has long claws.
The claws help the sloth
to hold on to the tree.

claws

Sloths like to live in trees.
They eat the leaves
on the trees for their food.
Some sloths sleep in the day
and wake up at night.

Sloths are very slow.
They are not good at walking
on the ground.
But. . . a sloth is good
at swimming.

7

A sloth is not good
at cleaning its fur.
Sloths can have mould
in their fur.
They can have bugs and
moths in their fur, too.

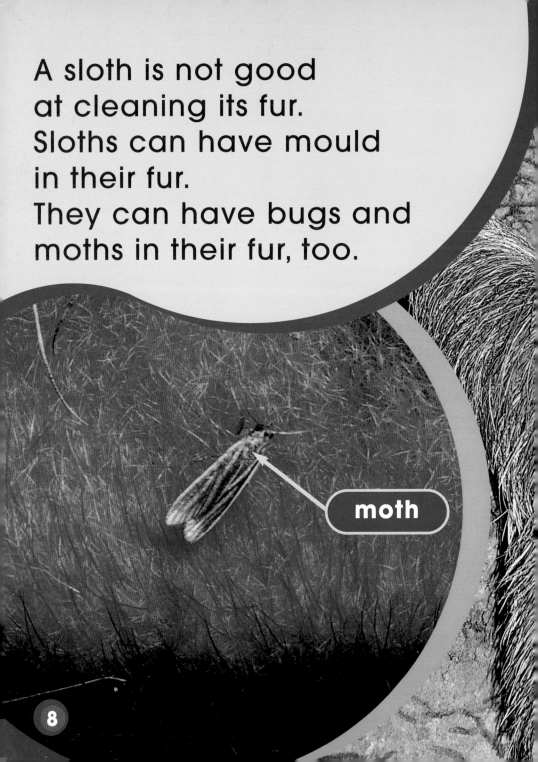

moth

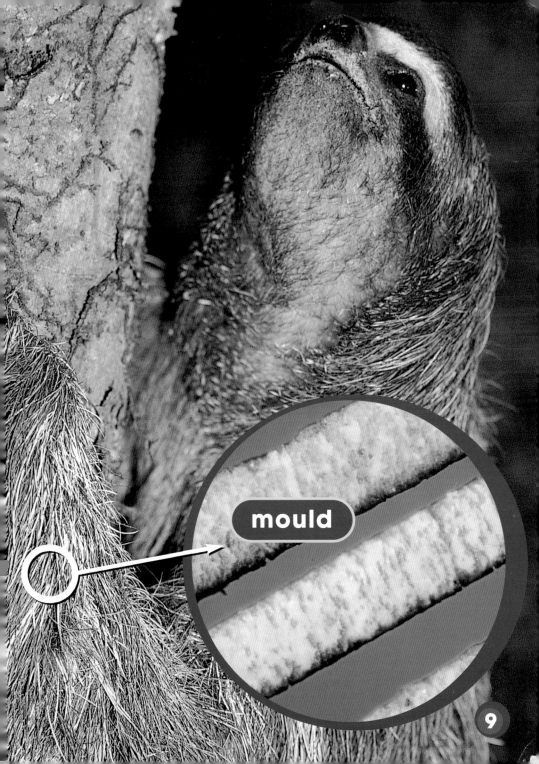

mould

A sloth goes down
to the ground to do
its droppings.
The moths lay eggs
in the droppings.
Little grubs come
out of the eggs.
They will turn into moths.

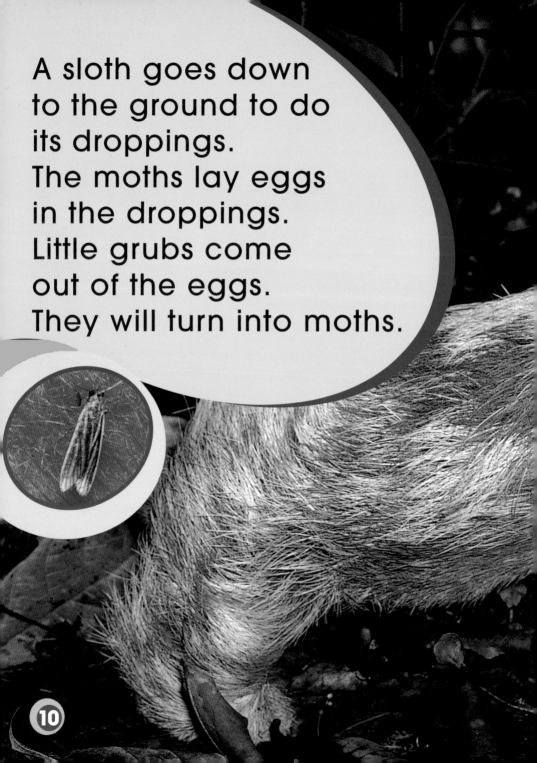

This is a mother sloth.
She has one baby.
The baby looks for
the mother's milk.
The baby stays
with its mother.

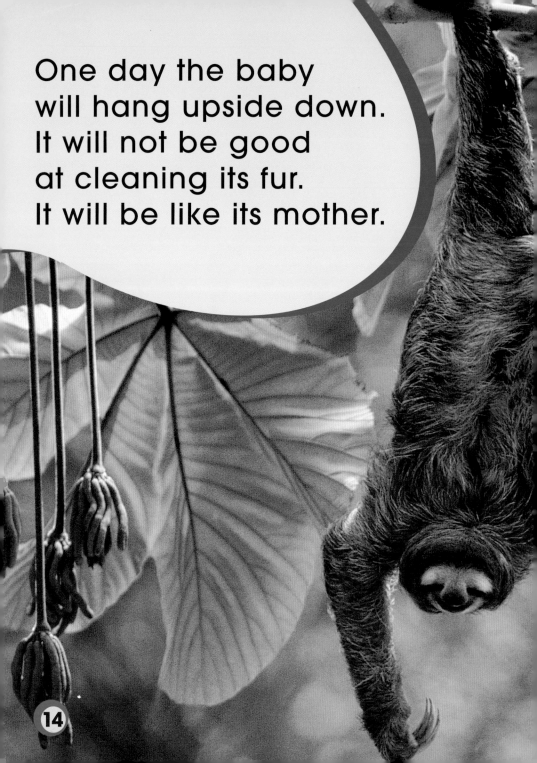

One day the baby
will hang upside down.
It will not be good
at cleaning its fur.
It will be like its mother.

Index

Guide Notes

Title: An Upside-Down Life
Stage: Early (3) – Blue

Genre: Non-fiction
Approach: Guided Reading
Processes: Thinking Critically, Exploring Language, Processing Information
Written and Visual Focus: Photographs (static images), Labels, Index
Word Count: 174

THINKING CRITICALLY
(sample questions)
- Look at the front cover and the title. Ask the children: "What do you think this book could be about?"
- Ask the children what they know about sloths.
- Focus the children's attention on the index. Ask: "What are you going to find out about in this book?"
- If you want to find out about what sloths eat, what page would you look on?
- If you want to find out about what sloths have in their fur, what pages would you look on?
- Look at pages 2 and 3. How do claws help the sloth to hold on tight?
- Look at pages 6 and 7. Why do you think sloths are not good at walking on the ground?
- Why do you think mould grows in the sloth's fur?

EXPLORING LANGUAGE

Terminology
Title, cover, photographs, author, photographers

Vocabulary
Interest words: sloth, claws, fur, mould, bugs, moths, droppings, grubs
High-frequency words: eat, day, their, very, goes, do, one
Compound words: upside, into
Positional words: down, in, on, upside down, out, into

Print Conventions
Capital letter for sentence beginnings, full stops, comma, ellipsis